australia

australia

a sense of place

foreword by sandy mccutcheon
photography by nick rains

VIKING
an imprint of
PENGUIN BOOKS

VIKING

Published by the Penguin Group
Penguin Group (Australia)
250 Camberwell Road, Camberwell, Victoria 3124, Australia
(a division of Pearson Australia Group Pty Ltd)
Penguin Group (USA) Inc.
375 Hudson Street, New York, New York 10014, USA
Penguin Group (Canada)
90 Eglinton Avenue East, Suite 700, Toronto ON M4P 2Y3, Canada
(a division of Pearson Penguin Canada Inc.)
Penguin Books Ltd
80 Strand, London WC2R 0RL, England
Penguin Ireland
25 St Stephen's Green, Dublin 2, Ireland
(a division of Penguin Books Ltd)
Penguin Books India Pvt Ltd
11 Community Centre, Panchsheel Park, New Delhi – 110 017, India
Penguin Group (NZ)
Cnr Airborne and Rosedale Roads, Albany, Auckland, New Zealand
(a division of Pearson New Zealand Ltd)
Penguin Books (South Africa) (Pty) Ltd
24 Sturdee Avenue, Rosebank, Johannesburg 2196, South Africa

Penguin Books Ltd, Registered Offices: 80 Strand, London, WC2R 0RL, England

First published by Penguin Group (Australia),
a division of Pearson Australia Group Pty Ltd, 2005

10 9 8 7 6 5 4 3 2 1

Cover & text design by Adam Laszczuk © Penguin Group (Australia)

Cover photograph by Nick Rains
Author photograph by Janelle Lugge
Printed in Hong Kong through The Australian Book Connection

National Library of Australia
Cataloguing-in-Publication data:

    Rains, Nick.
    Australia : a sense of place.

    Includes index.
    ISBN 0 670 02901 7.
    1. Australia - Pictorial works. I. McCutcheon, Sandy. II.
    Title.

    919.4

www.penguin.com.au

Nick Rains would like to express his appreciation to Fujifilm Australia for their ongoing support
and to Britz Rentals for allowing him to use their campervans whilst shooting images for this book.

contents

foreword by sandy mccutcheon vii

a sense of place

by sandy mccutcheon

... the whole appearance of nature must be striking in the extreme to the adventurer, and at first this will seem to him to be a country of enchantments.

Thomas Watling,
Letters From An Exile in Botany Bay,
To His Aunt in Dumfries, 1794

From the earliest days of European settlement through to the present, reaction to the Australian landscape has evolved from the initial sense of enchantment to which the painter Thomas Watling refers, to a more sophisticated appreciation and respect. Evident in the early paintings, limited as they were by the European eye and pictorial techniques, is an appreciable sense of bewilderment at the scale and diversity of what confronted the artist. There were few places where the new arrivals could feel at home. The dry sclerophyll forests of their new land must have seemed harsh and inhospitable – a world away from the deciduous forest glades of Europe with soft mosses underfoot and a promise of rain in the air.

Yet this landscape, which appeared so alien and confronting to the white settlers and explorers, had been home for thousands of years to Indigenous Australians for whom the plains, ranges and deserts were a sustaining, spiritual and integral part of their existence. To look at the gulf between Indigenous art and that of the Europeans is to sense the vast difference in how each sees the landscape and people's relationship to it. That such a gulf exists is understandable given that Aboriginal art is the oldest such tradition in the world, reaching back more than 40 000 years.

Browsing through a collection of early Australian paintings it is easy to feel that they offer us the perspective of an outsider looking in. When reading accounts of exploration or settlement the feeling aroused is often one of 'intrusion'. Many ecologists and Indigenous Australians would concur and indeed, flying over the continent, evidence of the European expansion unfolds below you as a series of scars and incisions upon an ancient and fragile environment.

Our national mythology has long been rooted in 'the bush' and, in the face of scientific evidence to the contrary, it has been rich soil well fertilised by folklore, painters and poets such as Banjo Patterson and Henry Lawson. As the settlers spread out across the new land they attempted to 'tame' the country, cutting down native trees and creating a landscape that – at least for a short time before salinity problems and loss of topsoil took their toll – resembled a more familiar European scene.

Australia is not an easy continent and our expeditions towards the centre have been (in the grand scheme of things) only minor incursions; as a people we have clung overwhelmingly to the fringes of the continent, clustering around the essential supplies of water and some of the most spectacular coastlines on the planet. As the years passed and the cities became the economic powerhouses, they also became

Butterfly Gorge, Northern Territory

magnets for those in rural Australia who were 'doing it tough'. Drought, salinity, fire and the changing economics of farming have all contributed to the slow demise of the country towns and the shift to the coast. Now our identity is largely defined by the city and the sea. The modern sea-change phenomenon has, contrary to what some might think, long been a part of the Australian dream.

Despite this move to the edge of the continent, the struggles of those in the bush have become iconic symbols of our nation and, if the politicians are to be believed, helped form our national character. However, the battlers who once resided in the bush are now just as likely to be battling with mortgages and social isolation in the outer suburban areas of our cities. The bleak urban mundanity captured in the works of artist Jeffery Smart, where the lone human figure is hemmed in by man-made objects and dwarfed by their surrounds, is the world in which many feel they now live. For all the inner city art works and fine architecture the urban landscape is far more fluid than that which nature continues to fashion in the hinterland. The city is a work in progress, torn down and rebuilt on a time scale we can comprehend. In a sense the cities are our escape from the wide brown land that exists for many only on the widescreen of their home cinema.

With the increase of urbanisation, many people have cut them-selves off from the Australian landscape. In our towers of glass, or neatly defined suburban blocks, we have the illusion of control. Air condition-ing can make us forget the heat of the day, and it is possible to spend the entire day in an artificial environment. Yet, though there is a growing drift (some would say, stampede) to the coast, the mythologising of the outback continues. It is a mythology that flies in the face of reality for, not withstanding the number of off-road vehicles in evidence on our city streets, very few have ever 'been bush'.

For a majority of Australians their relationship with the outback or further, the centre of Australia, is at best ambivalent. More than one writer has referred to 'the dead heart' of Australia and over the years it has proved to be much more than mere metaphor. Other than for Indigenous Australians, the harsh and unforgiving power of the Australian landscape demands respect, for, as the early European explorers and a number of more recent unfortunates have discovered, it is possible to perish very quickly if one is careless. The sheer distance, the lack of water and at times inhospitable climate all combine to create a sense in which the land becomes an adversary. From first settlement through to modern times our literature, folklore and newspapers have all recorded the tales of those who strayed too far into the bush, never to be seen again. In our collective imagination we store the images; bleached bones in red dirt, shrunken skeletal remains of cattle or sheep, the broken windmill and the vehicle that did not make it through the sunburnt country. Stories of lost children abound and when combined with flooding rivers or the horrors of bushfires contribute to a deeply-held fear of the natural powers that lurk in the bush.

Images of Australian landscape, in painting or photograph, soon disabuse the viewer of any remnant belief that humans are central in the scheme of things. And when we do venture into the landscape it is so often, like the early explorers and pastoralists, an intrusion that leaves us vulnerable. To contemplate the figures in Drysdale's 1947 painting *The Rabbiters* is to witness individuals psychologically alienated from a landscape that is as malevolent as it is uncompromising.

Yet there is another equally profound power in the Australian landscape that touches us in a more spiritual way. Its stark beauty, vastness and unforgiving nature is both uplifting and, at the same time, humbling. The power is so dramatic that its effects can be felt when contemplating such vistas in the work of an artist or photographer. There is no easier way to be reminded of one's own mortality than to gaze out over the seemingly endless salt plains of Lake Eyre. In that instance it is the distance to the horizon that reduces a human to a mere speck, but step into a pristine and primeval rainforest setting in North Queensland and it is the span of time rather than space that overawes. Rock formations, golden beaches and endlessly shifting dunes all inspire wonder and remind us of our own fragility.

The first photograph taken in Australia was in May 1841 but it was to be almost another hundred years before the landscape photographer came to the fore with the work of Harold Cazneaux and others in what was dubbed the school of 'Pictorial Photography'. The school believed that the photograph should go beyond a record of reality, and the camera become more than a functional tool. A photograph, they argued, should be a work of art. While the photographer Max Dupain acknowledged Cazneaux as the father of Australian photography, he belonged to the more confronting 'New Photography' movement who, with their dramatic use of extreme viewpoints and sharp focus, portrayed the human figure in heroic ways that owed much to the aesthetics of Soviet Realism.

After moving from New Zealand where he had been born in 1878, Harold Cazneaux studied at the Adelaide School of design with fellow student Hans Heysen. The painter's later work was to prove a major influence on Cazneaux who aspired to capture the constantly changing Australian light in a similar fashion. The results were impressive and possibly best exemplified in what many consider the quintessential image of Cazneaux's; a photograph, taken in South Australia's Flinders Ranges in 1937, of a gnarled and majestic gum in an ancient landscape. The resulting photograph, entitled *The Spirit of Endurance*, is extraordinary in its resemblance to a painting.

The aesthetic rather than utilitarian approach of the landscape photographer opens the image to individual intuitive understanding. On one level it is an historical record; a unique moment in time that existed only in the 125th of a second blink of the shutter. The interplay of colour and light is captured and it is to the alchemy of the moment we respond; a moment that has already ceased to exist. On another level the photograph becomes the conduit for all we bring to the moment; our individual reaction based on past experience with nature and with art. The ephemeral nature of the moment does not rob it of intrinsic value, for our response to the image links us with the landscape in a way that no written word can.

For those of us who live a major part of our lives in towns or cities with little more than a fleeting glimpse of the Australian landscape – and then often only through the window of a speeding vehicle – photography has the power to give us an experience of its diversity and grandeur. And it is often not until we do spend time contemplating landscape – connecting or re-connecting with it – that we realise how important it is. Such moments can be brushed over, flicked through and put aside, but they can, if we allow them, let us enter the landscape and be replenished.

One of the major powers of good landscape photography is its affinity with the way the human eye sees and reads a landscape. The format of Nick Rains' photographs reveals how aware he is of this affinity and how skilfully he uses it. There is less foreground and the main features of the images stretch out across the horizon where they are intersected by the sky. The much vaunted Australian light is used to full effect in his shots and at times it is the light that takes centre stage, as in his capturing of a sunset reflected in the surface of a lake. This is contemplative work and brings home to the viewer how deeply satisfying it is to immerse oneself in the viewing of a landscape and thereby enriching our own inner world. The eye of a skilled photographer also acts as an antidote to the oft heard complaint of those unfamiliar with the Australian landscape, that it is 'all the same'. The photographer's view of the world shows us the detail in a rock, the play of light in a gorge or, to use Thomas Watling's words, 'a country of enchantments' we might otherwise have missed, right before our eyes.

The constant use by photographers, critics and viewers of the word 'capture' in relationship to landscape photography brings us back to the earlier notion of the ephemeral nature of the moment. And 'capture' is an apt word in much the same way as the photographer's use of the term 'shot'. For there is much in the method of a landscape photographer that parallels that of the hunter. A few minutes earlier or later and the conjunction of light and shade, of cloud formation or coruscation on water, will be different or gone for ever. A few metres left or right or from a different vantage point can and often does make the difference between a merely competent picture and a great one.

Given the sorry history of human impact on the land it is to be hoped that the images captured here are not destined to be a record of the way things once were; an historical document rather than a source of delight that invites participation. For it seems to me that the ultimate compliment that you can pay to a landscape photographer after immersing yourself in their images is to close the book and, suitably prepared, leave your house and begin your own journey out into the landscape.

The Cazneaux Tree, Flinders Ranges, South Australia

new

south wales

australian ca

victoria

tasmania

S O U

th australia

weste

rn australia

northe

queensland

xii–1   Coastline near
Lennox Heads at dawn

3   Campbell's Cove and the
Sydney Harbour Bridge

4   Sydney Seacliffs

5   Curiosity Rocks, Lake Jindabyne

6   Three Sisters, Blue Mountains

7   Murrumbidgee River, Wagga Wagga

8   Tilba Tilba, southern New South Wales

9   Mundi Mundi Plains,
northwest of Broken Hill

10   Byron Bay Lighthouse at dawn

11 Sydney skyline from Birchgrove

12 Valley of the Waters,
Blue Mountains

13 Mundi Mundi Plains,
west of Broken Hill

14 Nambucca Heads

15 Sydney Opera House
and Harbour Bridge

16–17 Australian National Museum

19 View of Canberra, Lake Burley Griffin
and Parliament House.

20 Lake Burley Griffin, the Captain Cook
Memorial Fountain and the National Library

21 Parliament House

victoria

33 Countryside around Churchill,
Gippsland

34 Twelve Apostles, moonset

35 Cape Otway Lighthouse

36 Melbourne skyline

37 Melbourne, Rialto Building
and Princes Bridge

38 Federation Bells, Melbourne

tasmania

39 Whisky Bay, Wilsons Promontory

40–41 Lake Dove and Cradle Mountain

42 Bay of Fires region,
The Gardens, Binnalong Bay

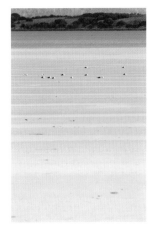

south ausralia

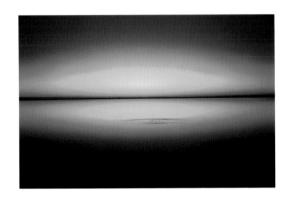

64   Kangaroo island

65   Dunes near Penong

66   Neales Creek, Lake Eyre

67   Lake Eyre, in flood

68   Lake Gairdner

69   Adelaide skyline

western australia

70   Eden Valley, Barossa Region

71   Remarkable Rocks, Kangaroo Island

72-73   Bungle Bungles, Kimberley

75 Moon over iron-rich Pilbara rocks

76 Perth from Kings Park

77 Kauri Trees, Pemberton

78 Fern Pool,
near Fortesque Falls, Pilbara

79 Elephant Rocks,
William Bay National Park

80 Summer storm over Merredin
wheatfields

81 Riding on Cable Beach, Broome

82 Knox Gorge, Pilbara

83 Mitchell Falls, Kimberley

84 Walpole, southwest Western Australia

85 Cape Leveque, Dampier Peninsula,
north of Broome

86 Purnululu National Park,
Kimberley (Bungle Bungles)

northern territory

87 Wandjina figures,
Mitchell Plateau, Kimberley

88–89 Kakadu National Park,
view from Obiri Rock (Ubirr).

91 Stuart Highway

92 Jim Jim Falls,
Kakadu National Park

93 Kata Tjuta, Kata Tjuta,
Uluru National Park

94 View of Alice Springs from Anzac Hill

95 Ghost gums of the
Western MacDonnell Ranges

96 Red dunes with goanna tracks,
northwest Simpson Desert

97 Old Telegraph Station, Alice Springs

98 Early morning mist near Cape Crawford

99 Yellow Waters Lagoon, Cooinda,
Kakadu National Park

100 Rock art, Nourlangie Rock,
Kakadu National Park

101 Uluru

102 Nourlangie Rock,
Kakadu National Park

103 Devils Marbles, Tennant Creek

104–105 Whitehaven Beach,
looking across Hill Inlet, Whitsunday Islands

107 Hook Reef,
off the Whitsunday Islands

108 The Chimneys,
Carnarvon Gorge National Park

109 Brisbane from Kangaroo Point

110 Fraser Island

111 Mossman Gorge,
Daintree National Park

112 Story Bridge, Brisbane

113 Hill Inlet and Whitehaven Beach,
Whitsunday Islands

114 Lamington National Park,
Binna Burra Section

115 Lawn Hill National Park

116 Horseshoe Bay, Bowen

117 Surfers Paradise

118 Near Innisfail, Far North Queensland

119 Windmills near Miles